Beautiful Souls

A tribute to the people who touch our lives in a special way

Compiled by Sam Choo

First Published 2023 by Hope Publishing

ISBN No. 978-981-18-7113-9

Contact Email: sam@hopepublishing.sg

Contents

Introduction

"Beautiful Souls: A Tribute to the People Who Touch Our Lives in a Special Way" is a heartwarming collection of stories penned by 14 talented authors, each sharing their personal experiences with the extraordinary individuals who have left an indelible mark on their lives.

These narratives celebrate the unsung heroes who have made a significant difference, not only to the authors but also to those around them.

From the inspiring tale of Big Jim, who transforms a timid child into a confident cowboy, to the unwavering support and love of a remarkable mother-in-law, each story offers a glimpse into the lives of these beautiful souls.

You'll find yourself immersed in stories of strength and resilience, such as a nurse's journey through cancer and gratitude, and tales of compassion, like a taxi driver's heartwarming pact to help those in need.

"Beautiful Souls" is more than just a collection of stories; it's a celebration of the power of love, kindness, and empathy. By providing us with role models who have made a positive impact on the world, this book serves as a testament to the enduring human spirit and the transformative power of connection.

Let the pages of "Beautiful Souls" inspire you to embrace the beauty within and recognize the remarkable individuals in your own life.

1

How Big Jim Turned a Mere Kid Into a Confident Cowboy

Kevin Riley

After moving from Switzerland, my family lived on a cattle ranch in Kamloops, British Columbia, surrounded by rolling hills, tall Ponderosa pines, and fields of alfalfa. My father was a cattle rancher, and we had over 300 head of cows, as well as about the same number of calves each year. It was a hard life, but a good one. Growing up, I learned how to work hard, and I also learned a lot from an old cowboy named Jim Kelly.

Big Jim was a fixture on the ranch, having worked there for as long as anyone could remember. He was a big, cheerful man with a battered and dusty brown Stetson forever perched on his head. Jim had seen it all and done it all, and he was always ready with a story or a joke. What I remember the most, and have always treasured about Big Jim was that he always treated me like an adult, a fellow cowboy, rather than the kid I was, and it gave me confidence.

Some of my best memories are of riding herd with Jim. Every spring, after the calves were born, we would brand them with the ranch's symbol, a 91. It was hard work, and it could be dangerous, but it was also a lot of fun. Jim would show me how to rope a calf and how to hold it down while it was branded. He was patient and kind, but he didn't coddle me. He expected me to work hard and to do things right, and I always felt proud when he praised me.

After branding, we would drive the cattle up to the rangeland, where they could graze all summer. This was my favorite part of the year. We would ride out early in the morning, before the sun had risen, and spend the whole day on horseback, moving the cattle from one high pasture to another. We would ride through creeks and over hills, dodging rocks and fallen trees. Sometimes we would see deer or coyotes, and Jim taught me many things about the native wildlife.

Jim taught me how to read the cattle, how to anticipate their movements, and how to use my horse to control them. He showed me how to use my lasso to catch a runaway calf, and he taught me how to swear like a true cowboy. I'll never forget the first time my mother heard me cuss my horse with a string of expletives that used just about every swear word in a cowboy's vocabulary.

Of course, life on a cattle ranch wasn't all fun and games. There were times when the work was hard, and the days were long. There were times when we had to ride in the rain or the snow, or when we had to deal with a sick animal or a broken fence. Jim never complained, though. He always had a smile on his face and a word of encouragement for me.

One summer, when I was about thirteen, we had a particularly difficult time. It was hotter than usual, and the grass was sparse. We had to drive the cattle high up into the very top fields of the rangeland. Our horses were tiring, wanting to return to the stables, and finally mine rolled on me. However, we had a job to do, and if Big Jim wasn't turning back, neither was After moving from Switzerland, my family lived on a cattle ranch in Kamloops, British Columbia, surrounded by rolling hills, tall Ponderosa pines, and fields of alfalfa. My father was a cattle rancher, and we had over 300 head of cows, as well as about the same number of calves each year. It was a hard life, but a good one. Growing up, I learned how to work hard, and I also learned a lot from an old cowboy named Jim Kelly.

Big Jim was a fixture on the ranch, having worked there for as long as anyone could remember. He was a big, cheerful man with a battered and dusty brown Stetson forever perched on his head. Jim had seen it all and done it all, and he was always ready with a story or a joke. What I remember the most, and have always treasured about Big Jim was that he always treated me like an adult, a fellow cowboy, rather than the kid I was, and it gave me confidence.

Some of my best memories are of riding herd with Jim. Every spring, after the calves were born, we would brand them with the ranch's symbol, a 91. It was hard work, and it could be dangerous, but it was also a lot of fun. Jim would show me how to rope a calf and how to hold it down while it was branded. He was patient and kind, but he didn't coddle me. He expected me to work hard and to do things right, and I always felt proud when he praised me.

After branding, we would drive the cattle up to the rangeland, where they could graze all summer. This was my favorite part of the year. We would ride out early in the morning, before the sun had risen, and spend the whole day on horseback, moving the cattle from one high pasture to another. We would ride through creeks and over hills, dodging rocks and fallen trees. Sometimes we would see deer or coyotes, and Jim taught me many things about the native wildlife.

Jim taught me how to read the cattle, how to anticipate their movements, and how to use my horse to control them. He showed me how to use my lasso to catch a runaway calf, and he taught me how to swear like a true cowboy. I'll never forget the first time my mother heard me cuss my horse with a string of expletives that used just about every swear word in a cowboy's vocabulary.

Of course, life on a cattle ranch wasn't all fun and games. There were times when the work was hard, and the days were long. There were times when we had to ride in the rain or the snow, or when we had to deal with a sick animal or a broken fence. Jim never complained, though. He always had a smile on his face and a word of encouragement for me.

One summer, when I was about thirteen, we had a particularly difficult time. It was hotter than usual, and the grass was sparse. We had to drive the cattle high up into the very top fields of the rangeland. Our horses were tiring, wanting to return to the stables, and finally mine rolled on me. However, we had a job to do, and if Big Jim wasn't turning back, neither was I.

That summer was tough, but it was also the summer when I learned the most from Big Jim. He showed me how to be tough, how to push through even when things seemed impossible. He taught me that being a cowboy wasn't just about riding horses and roping cattle. It was about being a good person, someone who could be relied on, someone who was honest and hardworking.

About Kevin Riley

Nowadays, Kevin Riley lives in the big city of Osaka – far away from his days as a cowboy. However, the lessons he learned from Big Jim have stood him in good stead throughout his life. As Big Jim was Kevin's teacher, so too Kevin has become a teacher. Find out more at https://ontrackwriting.comI.

2

Embers of Love: A Giant's Legacy

Patrick Chang

"On a poignant morning of July 16, 2020, we bid farewell to my cherished father, a memory that lingers like a never-ending dream. The previous day, I had paid him a visit, hoping to persuade him to consult a doctor. Unbeknownst to me, it would be our final encounter. As I departed, he uttered his last words: 'Make sure you eat well.' If only I had known, I would have stayed, sharing endless conversations."

The news of his passing left my heart in fragments. I endeavored to be strong for my family, but my inner turmoil remained hidden. Maintaining composure, I tried to stay occupied, but the moment I found solitude in the shower, tears cascaded relentlessly. The pain of losing someone so dear is beyond words.

My father's wealth was not in material possessions, but in the love and devotion he offered. He could not afford to give us everything we wanted, but he gave us all that he had. He bore our family's burdens, never voicing complaints or assigning blame. In the early 1970s, he ran a mobile drink stall outside a Katong cinema. The long hours he spent cycling between Norfolk Road and Katong left us with little time together, but when we reunited, joy filled my heart.

Eventually, he relinquished his mobile business and worked full-time as a delivery assistant at a textile shop, while also working at his cousin's clothing stall in the old Bugis area at night. With unwavering dedication, he provided for us, never expressing discontent.

Sunday mornings were cherished, as my father took my sister and me to a nearby playground. He watched us play with a beaming smile, masking any worries he harbored. On certain evenings, if he was free from the clothing stall, he would bring us to street hawkers, where we feasted on satay, chendol, and 'Dou Shuang,' engaging in lively conversation. These moments are forever etched in my heart.

The 1970s' Chinese Street Operas, or Wayang, held a special place in our memories. My father occasionally took time off to accompany us to the carnival-like atmosphere. On National Day, we watched the Wayang and marveled at the mesmerizing fireworks display. Our shared love for fireworks, perhaps inherited or inspired by him, endures.

A cup of coffee, a shared affinity between us, feels like a connection to him. In the late 1970s, my father embarked on a challenging venture, selling cassette tapes in a bustling Jalan Besar alleyway. Despite the demanding hours, he persevered, supported by my mother, to provide for us.

Unfortunately, trouble with an underground gang forced him to close the stall, leading him to work two full-time jobs, barely getting enough sleep, and sacrificing his own well-being for the sake of his family. We were concerned for his health, but he assured us that his colleague covered for him during the night shift, giving him an hour or two to rest. He told us not to worry.

The financial strain weighed heavily on him, but he remained optimistic, attentive, and caring for his loved ones.

Years later, with my National Service commencing and my mother securing a job, my father could finally leave the night shift. However, it wasn't until the early 1990s that our financial situation eased further, allowing my father to focus on his day job and take up cooking duties, expressing his love through simple yet delicious meals.

In 1995, my father's eligibility to withdraw his CPF savings presented an opportunity for rest and indulgence. Instead, he selflessly gifted his savings to us, enabling me to attend university and altering my life's trajectory. He continued working, refusing retirement, and always had a way of making us feel cherished and supported.

My father's unwavering positivity and humor remained despite life's challenges. He enjoyed anti-humor jokes, which my mother disapproved of, but we cherished. Even my son, born in 2009, appreciated his grandfather's wit.

In 2017, my father's health declined, and he eventually stopped working. Frequent clinic and hospital visits became a necessity, and we knew something serious was amiss. In 2018, upon his hospital discharge, we received the devastating prognosis that he had only two years left. Though surgery posed risks, we clung to the hope that he might defy expectations.

My father's indomitable spirit never waned. He fought valiantly, and for a time, his condition seemed to improve. We treasured every moment, acutely aware of time's fleeting nature.

However, on that fateful morning of July 16, 2020, the unthinkable occurred—my father passed away. The reality of his departure is still difficult to grasp. I deeply regret not taking my children to see him on July 15, thinking we had more opportunities. But those moments never came.

My father's memory may fade beyond my children's generation, but to those who knew and loved him, he was an extraordinary man—a devoted husband, loving father, and caring grandfather. His legacy persists in the values he instilled: diligence, selflessness, and the importance of family. As we bid him goodbye, I felt the enduring presence of his love and support.

His voice still echoes in my mind, reminding me, "When you cheat, you are not cheating others. You are cheating yourself!" This guiding principle encapsulates the essence of my father—a man of integrity, humor, and boundless love for his family. Though he stood at a mere 1.6 meters, he was a giant among men, possessing a soul of immeasurable beauty.

About Patrick Chang

Patrick Chang is an experienced independent financial consultant, with professional qualifications of CFP, ChFC, IBFA, and Certified Family Office Advisor. He is most recognized for investment portfolio construction, retirement design, and estate & legacy planning. He graduated with an MBA from the University of Adelaide and is also a certified DISC FLOW trainer for corporations.

Connect with Patrick via LinkedIn:
www.linkedin.com/in/patrickchang-pf

Email: askpatrickchang@gmail.com

3

The Mountains That Carried Me

Faranaz Mahmood Khan

It is often said that cats have nine lives, but in truth, they have only one, just like humans. Our lives are shaped by the environment we grow up in and the people who surround us. These individuals inspire, motivate, and encourage us to become the best versions of ourselves. For me, the people who have had the most profound impact on my life are my parents. Their unwavering dedication, support, and love have shaped the person I am today.

I am fortunate to have had both my parents present since the day I was born, which I know is not always the case for everyone. They have devoted their lives to raising my siblings and me to the best of their abilities. They may not be perfect parents, but their daily goal is to help us become kind, resourceful individuals who can make a positive difference in the world.

My parents are simple people who got married and began their lives together in Bedok, Singapore. They later moved to Tampines New Town, where I spent most of my childhood. Born in the 1950s and 1960s, my parents experienced the early years of nation-building in Singapore. They each had their share of struggles growing up, but they worked tirelessly to give my siblings and me a better life.

My father, Mark, believed that knowledge is power and would constantly buy books for us to read. I became an avid reader, finding solace and adventure in the pages of those books. This love for learning, coupled with my father's guidance, instilled in me a determination to achieve a university degree and fulfill his dream for me.

My mother, Balqis, emphasized values and discipline, teaching us responsibility, care for others, selflessness, and compassion. Her dedication as a homemaker and her unwavering love for us were unparalleled. She maintained a strict household to keep us focused on our goals and prevent us from going astray.

As I grew older, I came to appreciate the sacrifices my parents made and the lessons they taught me. I am grateful for their support, which has allowed me to achieve independence, a degree, a stable job, and a master's degree later on. But, more importantly, their teachings have shaped me into a kind, compassionate, and strong-minded individual who is determined to make a positive impact on the world.

My parents are the mountains that have shaped and carried me through life. Their love and support have been unwavering, even as my siblings and I have grown into adults with children of our own. The lessons they have taught me will forever be etched in my heart, and I will always be grateful for their presence in my life.

Here is a short poem I dedicate to them and all other beautiful parents out there!

Dear Mother,
There will never be another,
The love you gave,
I can never erase.

Dear Father,
It's just you and no other,
You fill my life with rejoice.
You bought me books and toys.

O Parents, indeed!
You were the mountains that carried me.
For your sweet dedication and eternal love,
I will indeed stay dutiful and serve you, you'll see.

O Parents, this is so hard!
One day, I know we'll be apart.
Time here is but a test in the blink of an eye.
But wait for me on the other side!

On the path of the marvellous gardens,
On the banks of gorgeous heavens.
Call out to me if you don't see me.
We will be reunited again, eternally.

About Faranaz Mahmood Khan:

A connoisseur of the finer things in life, she enjoys works of literature in English, fine poetry, and theater. Beach walks, countryside strolls, and mountain treks are her favorite activities when she travels overseas. An educator by profession, kindness and compassion are values she lives by and tries to instill in the children she meets. Possessing a wild heart and a constant daydreamer, she lives in the ideals in her head. On carefree days, she loves writing, cooking, reading, cycling, and learning new things such as baking gluten-free or sourdough bread. She has also enjoyed doing editing and copywriting for her friends.

Social media links:
https://www.instagram.com/nat_fara
https://www.facebook.com/natdia.faranaz

4

A Remarkable Mother-in-Law: An Ode to My Unconditional Supporter

Chrisco Neo

When I was first welcomed into my husband's family, I had no idea just how much of an impact my mother-in-law would have on my life. She was an ordinary woman, but extraordinary on the inside. Despite the many challenges she faced in her younger days she still managed to find a way to succeed in her studies, and provide for her family.

A few years ago, she was diagnosed with breast cancer but that didn't stop her. She tackled the painful journey of chemotherapy head on and managed to push through. Not only that, but she was also extremely resourceful when it came to finding solutions and answers.

My mother-in-law taught me how to be patient and how to handle difficult people, as well as how to overcome my own obstacles. I was also able to learn some special dishes that have been passed down through her grandmother.

She was always encouraging of us and never put us under any pressure, even when we faced our own challenges. She had such a close relationship with my husband that they could talk till the wee hours of the morning.

My mother-in-law has made a lasting impact on my life. There will always be something new to learn from her and I am so grateful that I have been given such an amazing mother-in-law, grandmother and wife.

She has been a reminder to me that it is never too late to learn, and that even the toughest challenges can be overcome. I am thankful for all of the support she has given us and for the special bond she has created with my husband and I. To my mother-in-law, I want to say thank you and I love you.

About Chrisco Neo

Chrisco is a wife and a mother of two lovely boys. Based in Singapore, one of her dreams is to help all parents have a better relationship with their next generation. As a positive parenting advocate, she shares the importance of building better relationships between parents and children. Moreover, she is also a computer consultant who aims to make laptops affordable for every household.

Links to her social media profile and website are provided below:

Facebook: https://www.facebook.com/chrisco.neo

Website:
http://www.computersformoms.com?ref=32

5

A Blessed Life

Samuel Sham

On a Saturday evening in August, a child was born at GH Kuala Lumpur. While every day sees new births, Samuel Sham was destined to stand out from the crowd.

Growing up in a kampong opposite Sungai Wang, life was different. But a fire changed everything and Samuel moved to the city life of Jalan Sungai Besi. Where the highway now cuts across and a massive 40-story building stands, once there were only memories of a simpler time.

Growing up

Growing up, he was always sickly, frequently struck down with high fevers that fried his brain. His mother never expected much from him, believing he wouldn't last long due to his health. She was just grateful he was alive, and every new year, she thanked God for her son's survival. To make matters worse, as a left-handed boy, he was stigmatized as less capable.

At the age of five, he fell down a flight of stairs, tumbling down 15 steps. Though he survived, the incident left him with a fear of heights and people. At ten, he was knocked down by a motorcycle, breaking his left arm into three pieces and leaving the arm with little strength or use. And at fifteen, he was hit by a car, suffering broken ribs and the loss of two front teeth. His life was a series of accidents, and fear built up within him, leaving him with very little confidence in himself or his abilities.

He struggled to put on weight and remained skin and bones, afraid of speaking up or interacting with others. He didn't excel in school, with every subject, especially math, being his worst. He wasn't good at sports or socializing and never took a leadership role in anything. He couldn't even sell a cookie to himself. Despite all these setbacks, he remained determined to turn his life around and find success in his own way.

After 60 Christmases, everything has changed. Cartwheels have given way to car wheels, and house phones have been replaced by smartphones. What once cost 20 cents now sells for $6.20.

But amidst all the changes, one thing has remained constant: his determination to succeed. He joined the Boy Scouts and became a kind scout, earning two degrees in the USA and paying his own way through university. He saved enough money while working in the USA to travel solo to Europe and backpack for six months. He chose a career in accountancy and management, selling life insurance part-time to learn the art of selling.

For 25 years, he ran a youth program, and helped to run an orphanage that housed 100 children. He served as a CEO of a trust company, leading a team of 50 professionals. He ran marathons and hiked mountains, completing 2 marathons a year and hiking Mount Kinabalu 9 times.

Nowadays, he speaks regularly, giving public presentations and motivational speeches. In fact, his current vocation requires him to do so regularly. He's a member of Toastmaster International, having earned his DTM in 2019. He serves on the board and exco of YMCAKL, and is the treasurer of an orphanage, Desa Amal Jireh. Despite all the obstacles he faced growing up, he has become a successful and accomplished individual, dedicated to making a positive impact on the world.

He credited the following people for shaping his life.

1. Ee Khoo

EE Khoo was my dad's second sister, and when I was between the ages of 7 and 11, my parents left me in her care while I finished primary school. For those five years, she treated me like a precious gem, always giving me her best. Even though I hated school, she never let that affect me. Instead, she would always encourage me to look at things in a positive way.

Whenever I said I couldn't do something, she would respond with "have you tried?" She wouldn't let me give up without at least attempting something first. She made sure to attend every event in which I participated, whether it was playing soccer, participating in sports day, or even a debating competition. I don't recall ever winning anything, but her presence and smile kept me motivated to keep trying. This instilled in me a DNA to try anything, even if the success rate was low. I became a risk-taker, always willing to try even if the chances of success were slim.

Sadly, EE Khoo passed away when I was only 30, but her encouraging smile remains with me to this day. Whenever I feel discouraged, I remember her and whisper a word of thanks. I dearly miss her, and every time I pass by the area where she lived, I pay my respects and express my gratitude for her impact on my life.

2. My Mother

It's difficult to do justice to my mum's impact on my life in just a few words, but I'll try to keep it brief. My mum was an uneducated vegetable seller in Central Market (now an iconic historic place for tourists). She didn't expect much from me due to my frequent high fevers, and she once told me that she didn't expect me to live past the age of 10. But by my 11th birthday, she knew I would survive.

My dad gave me a fountain pen, and I moved out of my aunt's home to live with mum and dad in Brickfields. I started secondary school there, and my siblings were my elder sister and younger brother.

From a young age, I saw money as a means of getting what I wanted, so I was willing to do anything if I got paid. During my Boy Scout days, I loved Job Week, where we would go out into the neighborhood to do odd jobs and get paid. We were always proud to be the top earners in the troop, and many times we were rewarded with an announcement in school assembly. Although the money didn't go to us, we felt good about being trusted with a task and completing it with pride. This instilled in me a belief that hard work doesn't kill anyone, and that the way to earn is to work hard.

Mum knew I was willing to work hard, so she offered me the opportunity to help her out in the market. Her condition was that I had to wake up at 3 am and leave home at 3.30 am with her, rain or shine. She wouldn't wake me up, so I had to make sure I was ready on time. I got paid $5 and another $10, which had to go directly into my savings. For breakfast, I could eat anything I chose. My bus fare home was $0.5 cents, and I walked the rest of the way home, stopping by the post office to deposit the $10 before going home. I wasn't allowed to bring the $10 home and go back later to bank it, and to this day, when I've decided on a certain percentage to go into my investment pool, it's done the same day and rarely postponed until the next day after receiving my payment.

My mum taught me several modules of business strategy, and she has always been my reference point when I need advice on business ventures. Her lessons have stayed with me, and her work ethic has been a driving force in my life.

Marketing 101

Despite running a small business of daily trading, my mum has never lost any money in her trading because of her ingenious formula. She's very focused and satisfied with the day's earnings, and she has a strict timeline for her work every day.

She buys vegetables from the wholesale market and times her purchases almost to the last minute before the transport leaves. The sellers get desperate because after the transporter leaves, the price will go down. Timing is important as she will not have to spend time negotiating if she turns up earlier, and most of the time, her offer is taken quickly. She pays in cash, which is a preferred term, and she starts the day with a good purchase from a bargain.

Time Vs Opportunity 101

My mum's business strategy is all about maximizing her time and opportunity. She sells quickly to earn her cost and as soon as the cost is achieved, she sells it in bulk at a discount below her cost since this is pure profit. Earning fast is better than earning that takes more time, and her trading hours are limited from 7 am to only 12 noon, which is five hours. After 12 noon, she outsources to her fellow colleague the leftover produce that is willing to stay till 5 pm. Her colleague has no cost on this produce, and all earnings are split 50/50. She either throws those leftovers away or earns a 50% profit without any effort.

She'd rather earn 50% than spend another 5 hours at the market, which she prefers to avoid. Instead, she heads back home to resume her duty as a mother to her children and get to bed early to start another day of trading. This way, she maximizes her time and opportunity and keeps her business running efficiently.

Property investment 101

When I got my first stable job, my first investment was a car. My mum wasn't impressed with my decision and brought me to look at a property costing $47,000. I told her I couldn't afford even 10% of it. She then offered to loan me the money and with the rental income, I could pay off the property. After 10 years, I sold the property for $150,000, which was a significant profit. This was my first investment, and it taught me the difference between buying to invest and buying to reside.

My mum has an amazing wealth of knowledge about investing, which she considers common sense. I often have to reference material to prove that what she taught me is now being taught in business schools.

3. YMCA, Kuala Lumpur

The YMCA in Kuala Lumpur holds a special place in my heart. It provided me with a safe haven from the vices that surrounded me in my neighborhood. When I was just 12 years old, I would drop off my school bag at home and spend the rest of my days at the YMCA, located just 300 meters away. I knew I had to be home before my dad arrived at 4:45 pm, or else I would have some explaining to do. But even with the strict curfew, the YMCA offered me a sense of security and freedom that I couldn't find elsewhere.

I roamed around the YMCA, playing in the field, and sometimes, I was even offered food and drinks. As a young boy who was always hungry, I never refused. I knew I wanted to give back to this place that had given me so much, and eventually, I did. Today, I serve as a board member, executive committee member, and Membership Chairperson. I encourage other young people to find refuge at the YMCA, just as I did.

The YMCA was also the place where I was exposed to Christianity and started my search for truth. While I am not a religious person, I am a truth seeker. The YMCA provided me with a safe and nurturing environment, and I will always be grateful for that.

4. Rev Terrance Sinnadurai

Rev. Terrance Sinnadurai was more than just a spiritual leader to me - he was my first boss and mentor at Bible College Malaysia. He is a man of great character and compassion, who has dedicated his life to serving others. As the pastor of Kajang Assembly of God, he always took a personal interest in getting to know those around him, focusing on who they were as individuals before anything else.

It was this approach that drew me to him and his work, which included co-founding an orphanage with his wife Kamala over 45 years ago. Even now, the home they started, which can be found at www.daj.org.my, continues to give children a second chance at life.

Rev. Sinnadurai's organizational skills were also impressive. I remember him always carrying around a folded A4 paper, with one half dedicated to his personal errands and the other half for work-related tasks. He would check off each item as he accomplished it, setting an example for me that I still follow to this day.

But more than anything, Rev. Sinnadurai was always there for me, offering a listening ear and practical advice whenever I needed it. He never pushed his opinions on me, but always provided guidance when I asked for it. It's been over 20 years since I started working with him again, this time as a treasurer and board member for the orphanage. And even now, I still consider him a father figure in my life, who has given me countless second chances to succeed.

5. Mr Foon Wong

Mr. Foon Wong began his career as the manager of Chinese Chef, but to those who knew him, he was much more than just a boss. He had a likable personality that drew people to him, and he always went out of his way to make everyone feel welcome.

One of the things Mr. Wong was known for was his weekly home-cooked meals, which he would invite all the Chinese foreign students to attend. He was always generous, loaning out his car to help people move and even providing free chicken wings to the students, which became a staple of their diets.

I had the privilege of working with Mr. Wong at his restaurant, and he was always willing to give me extra hours during the summer when I needed the work. He even invited me to live in his home and share a room with his high-school brother, Philip Wong. He only charged me a token amount for rent, which saved me a lot of money on accommodation during my four years in the USA.

When I asked Mr. Wong why he was so kind to foreign students like us, who would eventually leave and have no way to repay him, he told me a story. When he was on Pulau Bidong, a refugee from his home land Vietnam, a Malay man helped him, and asked that he repay the favour by helping at least two people who had no way to repay him. Mr. Wong took this to heart and has helped countless foreign students over the years, without expecting anything in return.

Even after 32 years, I was able to catch up with him in Los Angeles, and I was pleased to see that he still carried on his mission to help those in need. His generosity has inspired me to do the same, and on every birthday, I make it a point to give to someone who cannot repay me. It has taught me that being blessed is not about accumulation, but about having a grateful attitude. Mr. Wong's impact on my life has been immeasurable, and I will always be grateful for his kindness.

6. My American Buddies

I consider myself incredibly fortunate to have friends who love and support me, even though they are not from my home country. During my 4.5 years in the USA, I was blessed to meet Ernie Taber, my first roommate who is now a retired PE coach, Doug Green who is now a pastor at North Hills Church, Barry Corey who is now Dr. Barry Corey and the President of Biola University, and Mike Leahy, a well-known movie director.

Ernie was the one who introduced me to American football, which I initially mistook for soccer. He also introduced me to Dr. Pepper, a soda drink that was more popular than Coca Cola. To commemorate our good times, I recently bought a 6-pack of Dr. Pepper for the new year.

Ernie would often take me home to Taylor, Michigan for Christmas, Thanksgiving, and Spring Break every year, and Doug's family lived on a farm in the southern part of Springfield where we would frequently hang out. Barry hailed from Boston while Mike was from Ohio, and through their influence, I took up representative positions in the Student Council and became the Deputy President for International Students. As a Business major in Accounting and Management, their friendship helped broaden my horizons and shaped me into who I am today.

Even after 35 years, we have remained in contact, and their impact on my life continues to be immeasurable. I will always be grateful for their love and support, no matter where I am in the world.

7. Raymond Tan

Raymond Tan was the one who sold me my first life insurance policy when I was just starting out in my career. As someone who was working in a corporate job, marketing and selling anything was a challenge for me. I had this preconceived notion that selling was difficult and not something I was cut out for, which is why I preferred to work on back-end processes.

However, Raymond introduced me to the tools of selling and coached me through the process of selling insurance, which is more about selling an idea than just a piece of paper. He supported me every step of the way, and slowly but surely, I became more comfortable with it. I even began to enjoy it, especially when I saw the money coming in.

I kept insurance sales as a side hustle and never thought of making it into a career, but through it, I developed my sales process and realized that I was more of an extrovert than I thought. I began to focus more on business development than back-end work and discovered that a desk job was boring for me.

I recently attended Raymond's birthday and was pleased to see that he was doing very well and had even spun off many agencies. I owe my confidence in selling to him, as now I am able to sell almost anything with ease.

8. Johnny Tan

Johnny Tan was my classmate and a dear friend who unfortunately passed away two years ago. I was privileged to present a eulogy at his funeral, where I shared how he came from a poor family, and his father was a bus driver. Despite the odds, he excelled in our secondary school's bookkeeping class, and even the teachers sought his opinions. Johnny worked his way up the corporate ladder, without the opportunity for tertiary education.

Despite the lack of formal qualifications, he earned the respect of top professionals within his company and ranked equally alongside them. He was always focused and willing to work hard, and his problem-solving skills were second to none. During a recession, when banks were recalling corporate loans, his company was among the few that convinced the banks to delay the recall, allowing them to pull through the tough times.

When I was heading towards a stable corporate job, Johnny told me that I was on the wrong path because I had many years ahead of me, and spending the next 30 years in the same company would not be fulfilling. He encouraged me to take some risks and venture out. His advice and guidance allowed me to spread my wings and take on a challenging role in a small developer company. Through his counsel, I learned how to survive and thrive in the corporate world.

Johnny's secret to success was simple - as long as you remained needed and willing to solve problems, you would always be welcome in your organization. In my later years, I became the CEO of a public trustee company, managing three more subsidiaries as the trouble-shooter. Meanwhile, Johnny retired at the young age of 40 and became a developer, building a hotel and apartment block from scratch.

At his funeral, I was privileged to share with his family that his wealth came from his hard work, dedication, and willingness to solve problems. Johnny may no longer be with us, but his legacy of hard work and perseverance lives on.

9. God

The most significant aspect of my career and life is my faith in God. I surrendered my life to the Lordship of Jesus when I was just 16 years old. Life hasn't been easy since then, and I still face many challenges, but when I look back, I feel blessed.

There have been many unanswered questions and prayers in my life, but as I look at it through the lens of God, I realize that it is He alone who has brought me this far. My life began with many setbacks, but I am grateful for the people who have encouraged me, offered me wisdom, and favored me, which kept me moving forward.

I do not know when my journey will end, but whatever time is left, I want to spend it leading others to know His Lordship. I hope that whoever I meet will be able to see their life through God's lens too. As the Psalmist says, "I was young, and now I am old, yet I have never seen the righteous forsaken or their children begging bread." (Psalm 37:25)

For me, a life well spent is one that is given to a cause that has eternal value. On that faithful day, I hope to hear the words, *"Well done, good and faithful servant. Come and share your master's happiness"* (Matthew 25:21).

About Samuel Sham

https://www.linkedin.com/in/ficusavenue/

6

Embracing the Beautiful Soul

Agnes Koo

In a world where beauty is often equated with appearances, the concept of a beautiful soul transcends that superficiality. This is a story about my brother, a person with a beautiful soul, who shaped my life even after he left this world 15 years ago.

A beautiful soul, like my brother, embodies kindness, generosity, authenticity, balance, and understanding. They bring a sense of safety and peace to those around them. My brother's unique talent was his ability to learn anything in mere minutes. He began working at the tender age of nine, a common practice at the time, at our aunt's coffee shop in Kampung Malaysia.

Our family of seven siblings lived modestly, with each day bringing uncertainty about our next meal. Despite our circumstances, my brother thrived, mastering the art of making Dim Sum and Chinese

Steam Buns by the time he was 12. He eventually returned to our hometown, working as an assistant in a restaurant's Dim Sum department. There, his love for food led him to create numerous dishes, boosting his boss's sales and earning his admiration.

At 21, my brother embarked on a journey to Japan, where he immersed himself in the culture, language, and cuisine for five years. He returned home a changed man, and his beautiful soul inspired me to follow his lead. His bravery and drive to explore led me to Singapore, where I learned English, Mandarin, and Hokkien, eventually becoming fluent in six languages.

As I navigated life's challenges, I drew strength from my brother's spirit. I learned how to cook and manage a household, eventually earning my certificate in Singapore and charting my own path. Despite my father's insistence that I work instead of study, my brother's beautiful soul encouraged me to see education as a gift and to create my own life.

My journey led me to the world of internet marketing and social media, where I faced new challenges and learned from my mistakes. Like a stone becoming a diamond, I became a more beautiful soul. I now surround myself with positivity, blocking out the negativity that once hindered me.

Though my English may not be perfect, I've embraced the mantra: "If you want to do it, just do it." And so, I became an entrepreneur and coach, supporting my business partners in various ventures.

My brother's beautiful soul remains with me, a guiding light that has turned the impossible into possible. I have learned to appreciate the peace and beauty in the world, choosing to surround myself with positive energy and refusing to let negativity seep in. My brother's beautiful soul has become my compass, leading me through life's challenges and helping me create my own beautiful story.

About Agnes Koo

Agnes run a business that deals with AI trading, selling used laptops, making social media games, and affiliate marketing. To connect with her, visit her Facebook page:

https://www.facebook.com/agneskoo5563

7

Rides of Compassion: A Taxi Driver's Heartwarming Pact

Surina Sulaiman

Thirteen years ago, when my children were 2, 3, and 7, my husband was stationed overseas for several months. Mornings during the week were perpetually chaotic: rousing the children, bathing them, ensuring they brushed their teeth, dressing them, preparing bottles for the youngest two, and whipping up a quick breakfast for my eldest and me. To make it to work on time, I'd catch a cab to drop them off at my parents' house before rushing to the office.

On occasion, the heartache of separating from my tearful children was overwhelming. I'd contemplate waking up an hour earlier to save on transportation costs by taking a bus or squeezing onto the crowded MRT, only to revert to my initial plan for a few extra minutes of sleep.

As a working mother of three, I knew there was no perfect solution. I might arrive punctually, only to find forgotten bottles of milk in my bag. Or, after a dramatic departure from home, I'd realize how late I was for work while driving on the ECP. The elusive work-life balance seemed unattainable for working mothers like me.

One particularly difficult day, I had neglected to pack extra pocket money for a school trip and had yet to complete an urgent report for work. To make matters worse, I'd forgotten to order curry puffs for a family gathering that evening. Overwhelmed with stress and fatigue, I broke down in tears in the backseat of the taxi. The concerned driver inquired if I was alright and offered help. I wiped my tears and assured him it was just one of those days.

He reminded me that this, too, would pass. We sat in silence, interrupted only by the sound of taxi pickup requests, which he declined one after another. Then, he eagerly accepted a request for an advance booking to Singapore General Hospital (SGH) from Paya Lebar. Curious, I asked why he had declined a similar request but accepted this one.

The driver explained that he had three children around the same ages as mine. His wife had been retrenched eight months earlier and struggled to find work. They had been managing financially with dual incomes, but their recent difficulties revealed the challenge of supporting a family on a single income.

He longed to be generous but found it harder to give to charity or help those in need.

One day, he prayed for a way to continue giving and was struck with an idea. He vowed to provide free rides for any requests to a polyclinic or hospital, extending the offer to advance bookings. I asked him how many times he had done so, and he replied with a proud grin, "Three! And it felt amazing!"

I praised his noble act, and as we reached my workplace, we wished each other well. Although it has been twelve years, I will forever cherish the memory of that kindhearted taxi driver. His story reminds us not to fret over the little things and to always give back in whatever way our compassionate hearts allow.

About Surina Sulaiman

She is a part-time employee/entrepreneur, and a full-time mummy to three teenagers.

8

Endless Love

Carollyne Tong

The influence of a father in a child's life cannot be understated, as they offer guidance, support, and encouragement. A father's belief in their child can significantly impact their confidence and self-assurance. In honor of my late father, Steven, who passed away in April 2021, I dedicate this story.

My father was not an ambitious man, but he cherished his family. His career began in 1958 when he started working for his father's business, "Chuan Ann Shipping Company Private Limited". After his father passed away, the company closed down, and my father went on to work for his uncle, Tong Djoe, at "Tunas Group Pte Ltd." Tong Djoe, who had strong relationships with President Sukarno and Mao Zedong, played an essential role in diplomatic relations and trade between Indonesia and China. My father remained committed to this company until his retirement.

Throughout my life, my father has been a steadfast source of support. From a young age, he demonstrated his faith in my abilities and talents, providing me with strength, guidance, motivation, and inspiration. His words of wisdom and actions instilled in me a sense of confidence and self-belief that has helped me face numerous challenges and uncertainties.

COMMITTED PARENTING

My father had a passion for singing, and as a baby, he would sing me to sleep with his favorite pop songs, like "Sixteen Candles", instead of traditional lullabies. We were a family of five, and I had two younger brothers, six and eight years younger than me. My father made sure to take care of our emotional, financial, and practical well-being, working diligently to ensure our happiness.

He was a loving husband to my mother, always giving her his entire salary at the beginning of each month. My mother, content and happy, created financial stability through diligent savings. My father was also a caring and attentive father, actively participating in our upbringing and modeling respect, kindness, and responsibility. There are several special memories that the three of us will always cherish.

(1) Birthday Celebrations

What made our birthday celebrations unique was that our parents arranged for us to have our photos taken at a studio, dressed in our finest clothes, and seated next to our brightly lit birthday cakes. I still have these birthday photos, and they bring back sweet memories.

(2) School Days

During our primary school days, we were driven to school by a chauffeur. However, once I reached secondary school, I told my father that I felt embarrassed being chauffeured, so he took it upon himself to drive me to school every day. Despite having to wake up at 5 a.m., he never complained and made sure that I arrived at school on time.

(3) Fun at Movies

My father enjoyed watching movies and often took us along with him. Our record-breaking day consisted of watching three movies on a single Sunday. At first, we thought it was crazy, but we soon looked forward to our Sunday outings. To this day, watching movies remains my favorite hobby. We also have fond memories of attending the Jurong drive-in cinema, which was Singapore's only open-air drive-in cinema when it opened in July 1971. We would sit in our car, enjoying the movie along with mee siam and drinks. These experiences were unforgettable and brought immense joy during our childhood.

(4) First Color TV

When we got our first color television, we were so excited that I told my classmates, 'The Pink Panther is pink!' They thought I was bragging about our family's wealth, but the next day, they came over to our house to watch it.

(5) First Visit to KFC Restaurant

Our first visit to a Kentucky Fried Chicken restaurant was in Kuala Lumpur, Malaysia, as it was the first and nearest outlet to Singapore at that time. After that, my father would often drive us across the border just to have a meal at KFC. These trips were thrilling and memorable for us, as they also became opportunities for family bonding and exploration.

PROVISION OF RESOURCES

When I expressed my interest in learning the electone (electronic organ), my father supported me wholeheartedly. He bought me my first Yamaha electone, which cost about $5,000+.

I learned quickly and passed five grades in just six months. Seeing my potential, my father bought me an advanced Yamaha electone exam model that cost about $15,000+. I practiced very hard for six months and eventually earned my full Electone Teacher's grade. With this qualification, I was employed by Yamaha Music School as a full-time music teacher. My father's unwavering support helped me develop a deep love for the arts, and I had a successful music career. I also became a singer, recording artist, and vocal instructor.

BEING A GREAT LISTENER

My father had always been a great listener for my thoughts, ideas, and concerns. No matter how trivial they may seem, he always showed interest in my life, aspirations, and dreams. He was never judgmental or dismissive of my ideas. I enjoyed our father-daughter times when we talked about life for hours. He loved to share his past experiences, stories, and jokes with me.

DEMONSTRATION OF BELIEF

While I was studying for my G.C.E. 'A' Level at Temasek Junior College, I failed Economics in my first year. I had no interest in this subject and wanted to switch to another 'A' level subject, Chinese literature, in my second year. This meant that I had to cover eight short stories (first-year subjects) in addition to the second-year subjects, all in one year. Despite the challenges, my father never doubted my capability and supported my decision.

He believed that I had the ability to achieve anything I set my mind to and emphasized the importance of hard work and perseverance to me. As a result, I achieved a higher grade than I had expected for this subject.

UNCONDITIONAL LOVE

My father had never received much love and concern from his mother after his father passed away in his sixties. My grandfather was Indonesian and he married my Thai grandmother. He had three children with my grandmother and another five children with his second wife. My father, born in Indonesia, was the second eldest son and later became a Singapore citizen.

My grandmother did not approve of their marriage as my mother did not come from a wealthy family and was six years older than my father. Despite facing objections, my father showed unconditional love for my mother. They lived a wonderful life together and were almost inseparable.

When my mother was permanently disabled at the age of 78, my father became her caregiver for her daily living needs. During that period, I felt guilty for not being able to help take care of my mother as I was facing adversities and had to work very hard. However, my father reassured me that he would take care of her, which allowed me to focus on my work. Years later, when both of them were diagnosed with stage 4 cancer, my father continued to care for my mother despite his own condition. She was very dependent on him for her emotional needs and never wanted him to leave her sight.

What I believe is that my mother did not stand alone. The most potent force in her life was the love of her husband, which supported her through everything. My mother passed away at the age of 85, in the same month as my father, in April 2021, just 23 days apart. They were deeply in love until the very end of their lives, and I can feel the pain my father was going through when he lost her. In my book, "The Overcomers", I shared how I overcame the adversities of losing both of my parents.

Through my father, I learned about unconditional love. From what he had experienced, I understood that it was a painful and sacrificial way to love and care for my mother. It was much deeper than butterfly kisses, a steamy night of passion, or the joy children bring to their parents. My father's love for my mother was endless, until the day she passed away and forever in his heart.

FORGIVENESS & FEAR

I knew that my father's pain for me stemmed from his fears and concerns due to my past failed relationships. I had hurt and disappointed him, but I had never expressed any regrets. I felt that ultimately, I was the one who had to live with the consequences of my decisions and for not listening to his advice.

After my divorce in 2008, my father was fearful that I would enter into another marriage. There was a lot of tension when I had decided to marry my current husband, Hendri. My father preferred me to stay single and be happy. However, I believed in love and that I could find the right man to spend my life with. We had an open and honest conversation, and he finally understood my feelings and decision.

As my father forgave me, I also forgave myself and began working on my own healing process. I listened to my father's perspective and tried to understand his feelings. He may have been hurt, angry, or disappointed, and I needed to acknowledge and validate his emotions.

My father's love and support have left an indelible mark on my life. His dedication to our happiness, his unwavering belief in my abilities, and his endless love have shaped me into the person I am today. As I continue on my journey, I carry his wisdom, memories, and love in my heart, knowing that his spirit remains with me forever.

In conclusion, I am eternally grateful for the love and support of my father, Steven. His endless love and dedication to his family have left a lasting impact on our lives. Although he may no longer be with us physically, his spirit, love, and lessons continue to live on in our hearts and memories.

About Carollyne Tong

Carollyne Tong holds a Master's degree in International Business and a Bachelor of Commerce. She is a certified WSQ ACLP trainer (IAL), and a Style Coach. Her 'StyleShowing' program is a creative and engaging formula that enables clients to boost their self-confidence and self-esteem from the inside out. To know more about her and her work, connect with her at https://www.linktr.ee/carollynetong

9

The Healing Power of Love

Hendri Wong

I would like to share a story about the transformative power of love, inspired by the beautiful soul of my wife, Carollyne. She is like an angel who brought light into my life and saved me from the darkness. Her love has healed me, and I am forever grateful for her presence in my life.

My journey has been filled with struggles and hardships. I dropped out of school at a young age to support my family, and I have faced numerous challenges in both my career and personal life.

I got married in 1995 through matchmaking by a friend. My ex-wife was an accounts assistant, and I was a storekeeper working in Singapore Aerospace for 14 years until I was retrenched. After my retrenchment, I searched for jobs to support my family and was delighted when I found a position as a security officer. I was later promoted to security supervisor after a few years. Unfortunately, throughout our marriage, my ex-wife constantly belittled me and made me feel worthless. Our marriage ultimately ended in divorce, leaving me feeling lost and alone

But then, I met Carollyne. Her positivity and kindness were like a beacon of hope, guiding me out of the darkness. She was there for me when I needed her the most, offering me advice and comfort during my darkest moments. Her unwavering faith in God and her gentle spirit helped me find peace and purpose in my life.

Carollyne invited me to her church, and after a few months, I accepted Jesus Christ as my Lord and Savior. One year later, I was baptized in the church. I was transformed into a completely different person, and I learned how to manage my temper and emotions.

Through her encouragement and support, I discovered my strengths and passions and began to pursue my dreams. She helped me improve my mental state and even supported me financially during tough times. Her selflessness and generosity touched my heart, and I know that she was the one for me.

We fell in love and got married in 2019, and I have never been happier. Carollyne has shown me what true love and devotion are, and I am honored to be her husband. Her kindness, compassion, and forgiveness inspire me every day, and I am grateful for the lessons she has taught me.

arollyne has a beautiful soul, like an angel sent to me by God. I was touched by her kind heart, her love for me, and her compassion for those around her. Seeing these qualities in her made me love her wholeheartedly and want to take care of her.

- Carollyne has a kind and gentle heart. As she loved me, she also loved my late mother dearly. My late mother passed away in 2022 and Carollyne's support comforted my heart.

- Carollyne is kind and compassionate towards others. She always tries to put herself in other people's shoes and shows empathy towards their pain, difficulties, and struggles. I saw her true beauty shine through in her coaching sessions with friends and clients.

- Carollyne has an open mind and always ready to listen to others without judgement. She treats everyone with respect regardless of their age, race or social status.

- I admired Carollyne's generosity through her support for people, whether it is through a helping hand or giving something to those in need. She gives without expecting anything in return.

- Carollyne's kind character is infectious, and she always wears a warm smile. She loves to make others feel better, and people are naturally drawn to her authentic nature. She has a gift for making others feel seen, heard, appreciated, and loved.

- Carollyne possesses a forgiving and understanding heart. She believes in giving people second chances and willing to offer them help regardless of what happened in the past. Although she is forgiving, she also has the wisdom to choose the right relationship with people.

- Carollyne radiates positivity and often leaves an unforgettable impact on those around her. As her husband, she gives me encouragement and positive feedback in our daily life and business.

- One of the attributes from Carollyne that sets her part is her ability to see the good in others when they may not see it themselves. She helps them recognize their own potential.

- Another area in which I admire Carollyne is her positive attitude and mindset towards continuous learning. She never stops learning, and she believes that if she stops learning, she stops growing

What I admire most about my wife is her unwavering faith and spirituality. Her Christian disciplines and beliefs guided her in everything she does and she radiates light to others. Even when she was busy with work and family commitment, she continued learning business courses from the experts and also continued her Christian studies two years ago, which she achieved Bachelor of Theology degree.

In the world now where there is so much focus placed on material success and personal gain and interests, Carollyne is a shining example of living a life of true purpose and meaning. Her beautiful soul touches everyone she knows, and I feel grateful to have her in my life as a reminder of what is truly important in life.

As a couple, we strive to make our marriage a happy and fulfilling one. We have committed to the following ways to improve in our relationship. Here are some tips:

1. Communication

Communication is key to any successful relationship. Communicate regularly, openly and honestly. Listen to each other and try to understand each other's perspectives.

2. Respect

Respect each other's opinions, feelings and individuality. Treat each other with kindness, understanding and appreciation.

3. Resolve conflicts

It is inevitable to have conflicts in any relationship but it is important to resolve them in a healthy way. Active listening, compromising and showing forgiveness will help in resolving them. Understand each other's perspective, feelings and emotions.

4. Keep the romance alive

To make our partner feel loved and special, we need to keep the romance alive. Having gestures like cooking a favourite meal, planning a surprise date, buying a thoughtful present, leaving a love note or saying "I love you" are ways to keep the romance alive and make your partner feel wanted.

5. Quality time

Make time for each other and spend quality time together. It should be meaningful and enjoyable for both of you. It should add value and does not have to be something expensive.

6. Work as a team

Couples need to work together as a team to achieve their common goals and support each other in their individual goals. Constant encouragement and believe in the strengths of your partner is a good way. Whenever there is success, regardless whether it is small or big, always celebrate together. Partners should also be there for each other during difficult times.

Carollyne has shown me that true love is about more than just material success or personal gain. It's about family, personal growth, community and spiritually. Her unwavering faith in God and her commitment to living a life of purpose and meaning are a constant source of inspiration for me. I am grateful for my wife and the love she has given me. She is my queen, my mentor, my inspiration and the most important person in my life. With her by my side, I know that anything is possible.

About Hendri Wong

Hendri Wong is a health and wellness coach who specializes in effective detox and wellness programs. His focus is on achieving reverse-aging, promoting a "preventive measures" and "non-drug treatment" ideology, and helping people stay healthy while adding value to their lives. Learn more about him and his work by visiting his social media at https://linktr.ee/hendriwong.

10

I Believe in Angels

Dr Vivian Passion Koh

"I Have a Dream, a song to sing
To help me cope, with anything
If you see the wonder, of a fairy tale
You can take the future, even if you fail
I believe in angels
Something good in everything I see
I believe in angels
When I know the time is right for me
I'll cross the stream, I Have a Dream"

- *Song from I Have a Dream by Singer ABBA*

I love the song "I Have a Dream." When I think of the beautiful souls that I have encountered in my life, I can't help but first thank Father God for sending many "angels" into my life to help me cope with anything.

Angel of Great Love

The first beautiful soul that I encountered was my late mother. When she was alive, she was always very supportive in whatever I did, morally, physically, and financially. At my mum's wake in August 2022, during a quiet moment, I thought about her and her life journey. She showed me what true success is. I saw her dedicating her entire life to serving her family and 11 children until her last breath at the age of 88.

What was her achievement as a committed wife and caring mother? She left behind 79 descendants, including children, grandchildren, great-grandchildren, brothers and sisters-in-law, who loved her very much and accompanied her until her cremation. She was a great mediator when family members had personal arguments, and ensured the final outcome resulted in everyone coming together with gracious living and harmony towards every family member with love and care.

I am who I am today because of her unconditional love and support throughout my growing up journey. Her teachings and spirit of humanity will always be in my heart.

Angel of Understanding and Belief

My Olivia has started the single parenting journey with me at the young age of 18 months old. As much as I try my best to give her as much love and care as possible, deep down in my heart, I worry about her growing up with her peers when she sees her friends with a father and mother as a happy family, which I can't provide for her.

One day, I asked her how she felt without a father. She comforted me by saying that having me was more than enough. She gave me a hug and said, "Mummy, I love you." What a mature and understanding child I have, and I thank God for this precious gift.

There was one unforgettable, magical, heart-warming moment with Olivia when she was only 7 years old. She awarded me a trophy on June 9th, 2020 with the words "Noble Peace Prize" for my hard work at the Pay Kindness Forward movement. She witnessed me, during the Covid circuit breaker, enthusiastically educating and inspiring people over Zoom to join my movement to achieve the United Nations' 17th sustainable development goal with an intention to promote world peace and humanity through the goal of "Partnership".

My little angel, Olivia, said, "Mummy, even if nobody believes in you, I believe in you and whatever you do with a big heart." Her words melted my heart. At that moment, all the doubts and rejections I faced while pursuing my big calling felt worth it. My heart is full of gratitude to have this beautiful angel in my life.

Angel of Humanity and Support

I never expected that a meeting with Rendy to invite him to be my International Education Council (IEC) Angel for Philippine High School's student leaders would lead us to building a strong bond and working together for the betterment of humanity.

I remember on 30th Mar 2020 8pm when I launched the "United We Mask, United We Must" initiative. My pure intention was to educate people that wearing masks is an act of responsibility for both themselves and others. However, many concerned friends commented that it could cause doctors and nurses to have a shortage of masks. I felt very sad, realizing that it was not easy to even do good. I started calling him and cried as I wondered if my initiative was wrong.

Rendy's reply cheered me up. He said, "Vivian, you never saw how many times I cried in a corner for doing my 'Syncflow' work when I didn't get understanding from family and friends. Yet, I am a man. Just go with your flow. When you feel it's the right thing, just do it!" Immediately, I burst into laughter. Why? Because I wasn't alone and I was so grateful that Rendy shared his authentic self. With Rendy's comforting words, I charged ahead again...

Another support from Rendy was on March 30th, 2020 when I sent a Facebook messenger to our Education Minister, Mr. Ong Ye Kung. I was seeking his support for organizing Singaporeans to watch a movie called "Pay IT Forward" together as a nation so that we could understand the philosophy of Pay IT Forward. I had implemented the same concept with two passionate teachers, Jo Octavio, a 23-year-old science teacher, and Betsy Pearl Sucaldito Mambiar, a 49-year-old English teacher at Bulwangan National High School in the Philippines. That is where the IEC Visionboard movement was first born, on 30th April 2020.

Honestly, I didn't even know where this movement would lead to a year ago. I desired so much to help the students there with the dream board activity and let them know that whatever they drew, their dreams would come true. Now I realize that it was preparing me to jump the next hurdle.

Why do I believe in what I'm doing? I documented it in 2005 when I attended Steve Chen's program in Shenzhen. He asked us to write down what we desired 10 years down the road. Not able to predict my future, I just went with the flow. Today, when I look back, I'm already leading the life I always desired.

As for my bigger and bolder dream, I'm still on my journey of pursuing it...

On April 18th, 2020, I committed myself to the 21-day Abundance exercise facilitated by Rendy, which geared me up to the next level of 'SynchroDestiny' and gave birth to Pay Kindness Forward (PKF) on May 7th, 2020. The vision is "Pay It Forward + UN SDG 2030 = World Peace."

On June 6th, 2020, I spiritually confirmed the realization of my passion in the 17th UN's SDG, which is partnership to fulfill the other 16 SDG goals.

When I'm in doubt, Rendy is always there to affirm me. When I was stuck, he guided me to practice the 'Syncflow' movement. I made a breakthrough within minutes of Rendy showing me the Syncflow zone. I obtained the 'aha' moment, knowing where I am right now! This is simply amazing!

My favorite words recently are "BE THE CHANGE I WANT TO SEE IN THIS WORLD." If everyone just sows three seeds of kindness, the multiplying effect is enormous, and we have 356 days a year to make it happen. If you can change the world, will you?

I certainly can resonate with the SyncFlow zone created by my business partner, Synite Training's Mr. Rendy Tan Ravi. He has created a SyncFlow chart that allowed me to thrive in the self-realization and self-discovery journey that I have been searching for years.

Thank you, Rendy!

Angel of Community Building

Through my searching journey to make more impact for humanity, I am overjoyed and forever grateful to the universe for finally connecting me to one of my most important missing puzzles, Mr. Steven Koh, founder of Community of Learning (Singapore). He is passionate and an expert in community building, social learning, and business collaboration, and has further supported me in my PKF work. His willingness to allow me to leverage his talents, skills, experiences, and network gives me full confidence in working towards the UN2030 SDGs goal no. 17 and making it a reality both in Singapore and globally. Steven developed the roadmap to achieve the 16 SDG goals through Goal No. 17 Partnership, which connects all stakeholders together through community.

With Steven's leadership, Rendy and I have developed an excellent set of O3 programs to inspire individuals and organizations to overcome challenging VUCA (Volatility, Uncertainty, Complexity, Ambiguity) moments and receive abundant blessings through an open heart, open mind, and open will.

Conclusion

There are many more angels in our lives. They all contribute in their own unique way to us. I am forever thankful for them in enriching my life. I have a dream, and I believe in angels. They help us fulfill our dreams in life. How about you? Do you believe in angels? Who are your angels in life?

Dr. Vivian Passion Koh

Dr. Vivian Passion Koh is a serial entrepreneur with several education businesses, including Pay Kindness Forward, a global movement to inspire change and achieve sustainable development goals. Her mission is to connect, inspire, and empower people to pursue their passions with purpose, love, and gratitude. Contact her at:

Phone: +65 9693 7210.
Email: drvivian@firstclass.sg,

or visit the following websites for more information:

https://www.firstclass.sg
https://www.paykindnessforward.org

11

A Nurse's Journey through Cancer and Gratitude

Maureen Mok

I am a nurse who has been in the field for 26 years. I climbed up the ranks, but I found myself increasingly unhappy. I was in the midst of my Master's degree when I received a diagnosis that would change my life forever. I was diagnosed with cancer.

The news was a shock to me, and I was forced to reconsider what my priorities in life were. Suddenly the question "what if you only had one year to live?" was thrown right into my face. I was not prepared for a diagnosis like this. Before my diagnosis, I had a very toxic relationship with a certain family member. However, I made the decision to forgive this person for the hurt and anger caused to me. I realized that this was really FOR myself.

Cancer came as a blessing in disguise for me. It made me remove toxic people and cut away relationships that did not serve me anymore. It made me focus on the people who mattered to me. Before my diagnosis, all I could think of was work and studies, and my family and health took a back seat. But cancer made me appreciate nature and the little things in life that I had totally taken for granted. It made me remember to smell the flowers, look at my children, my mum and hubby, and my friends.

During my treatment, my sons accompanied me to my visits to the National Cancer Centre. I finally had time to chit-chat with them more and had nice breakfasts with them. And truly, laughter is the best medicine! But life should not be this way.

Prior to the diagnosis, I was a workaholic who pushed myself to the extreme. I could stay up all night to rush my assignments and the next morning, I went to work without any rest in between, or probably just one hour of sleep. Health was never a concern to me, and I was 41 when I got diagnosed. I recalled I was supposed to go for some health screening which I kept putting off. I had felt a lump but there was no pain, so I just ignored it. Till one day, I fell sick with flu and fever and had to go get some medication from my staff clinic. That was when I decided to tell the doctor about my concern. I was referred to the National Cancer Centre for further examination.

I can still remember my first consultation with my surgical oncologist. She called me to a corner after she examined me and told me chances are very high that it IS cancer. I was suddenly in a state of shock and almost disbelief. Long story short, my dear doctor immediately did the necessary to further confirm the diagnosis. She was my savior, she helped me fast-track many appointments, and within the next two weeks, I had started chemotherapy. The prescribed treatment for me included surgery, chemotherapy, and radiation. I just went with the flow and followed my doctor's instructions.

I lost weight and all my hair eventually, but looking good was important, so I made it a point to have my wigs and light make up. I still dressed up, in fact, I was happy with the weight loss! I did whatever I could to make the person in the mirror, that is myself, smile.

I got my insurance payouts, which came up to a handsome payout, but I could not enjoy it because of my current state of health then. My dear mum was very irritated with me when I still wanted to go back to work, and how I wanted to do most stuff on my own. She reminded me- what is the point of having so much money when your health is like that!? Suddenly I remembered I was so close to DEATH. Suddenly I prioritized MYSELF first.

I kept thinking of recovery and what I was going to do once I recovered. I had been thinking of going to Japan.

After I completed all my treatments, I brought my family, including my mum, to Japan. It was one of the best holidays we had. And I bought a nice SUV which served my family very well. When I talk to my friends, especially those who are not so young anymore, I reminded them to prioritize their health and well-being first. I often advised them to go for the necessary health checks.

I wanted to thank my company and fellow colleagues, the doctors, and my dear nursing colleagues and heads who showed their care and concern during this difficult time. I wanted to thank my Human Resource Department for being very supportive and helpful with my various requests- for my long absence away from work, for assisting with my requests for part-time work arrangements.

Through my cancer journey, I learned systems and hacks on how to leverage my time and influence to create passive income. My passive income has since exceeded my paycheck. I have made changes to my working schedule because I wanted more time with my kids. This is possible because I wanted it and I took the steps necessary to make it happen.

What I want to share is that we must have gratitude for everything that comes our way. Good things that happen are here to show we made the right choice and/or decision, and the not-so-good events are here to teach us a lesson. Learn from the lesson and do what is necessary before it is too late. I have since had friends who have been diagnosed with cancer, and I talked to them and kept infusing their minds with positive thoughts and beautiful dreams to look forward to. A few of them have since healed and are living a great life now.

You can be a victim of cancer, or a survivor. Cancer changes your life, often for the better. You learn what's important, you learn to prioritize, and you learn not to waste your time. You tell people you love them.

I am grateful for my life and the people who touched my life in a special way.

About Maureen Mok

Maureen is a nurse and a proud mother of four lovely kids. She is also a property investor and believes in living and loving life. Her journey of recovery from cancer has taught her to prioritize family over anything else.

https://www.facebook.com/profile.php?id=1384162217

12

Uncle Phillip: A Legacy of Belief and Inspiration

Kennedy Albar

"When life gets dark, that's when stars appear among us. Shine bright, beautiful ones. Throw light from your burning hearts."
– *John Mark Green*

Once in a while, life has a way of surprising us when we least expect it. For me, it was a transformative moment that changed my entire outlook on life.

Growing up, I knew I had potential inside me, something that could help me succeed in life. But the education system I was in focused solely on academic qualifications, and I struggled to keep up with my peers. My love for football didn't help, and my academic performance suffered.

Little did I know, God had a better plan in store for me.

Some would describe me as a man of few words. I have always believed in the power of silence, choosing to speak only when necessary and ensuring that every word I utter carries weight and meaning.

This way of life caught the attention of a man who would become a pivotal figure in my journey. His guidance and mentorship transformed me into the person I am today, and I will forever be grateful for his impact on my life.

Uncle Phillip was a remarkable man, full of charm and wit. As a close family friend, he was a frequent guest at our gatherings, and his presence always put me at ease. He had a unique gift for making everyone feel at home and igniting laughter with his quick wit and sense of humor.

To me, it seemed as though his wit and humor were as natural to him as the air we breathe. It flowed through him like blood in our veins, making him an unforgettable presence in my life.

Uncle Phillip's quick wit and charm led to a life-changing opportunity for me. During one of our family gatherings, he initiated a job offer that gave me a head start in my career and set me on a path to success.

As always, Uncle Phillip was engaging and captivating with his intellectual conversations and witty banter. During this particular gathering, we were discussing the art of presentation, and I shared my insights based on my knowledge and experience.

During our engaging conversation on the art of presentation, things got intense, and Uncle Phillip and I found ourselves in a spirited debate. Others around us took notice, viewing it as a lively and thought-provoking discussion.

What I didn't realize at the time was that our exchange of ideas had a profound impact on Uncle Phillip. I helped him view his business from a new perspective, and our discussion marked the beginning of a fruitful working relationship.

I was inspired by Uncle Phillip's passion for teaching, and he ignited a flame in me that burned long and slow. Through his guidance and mentorship, I discovered my own passion for teaching, and I am grateful for the impact he had on my life.

Under Uncle Phillip's mentorship, my career flourished, and I was presented with new opportunities that I never thought possible. For over a decade, I worked alongside him, growing and developing as a professional.

As I progressed in my career, I felt a calling to pursue a new path - that of academia. It was a challenging and daunting prospect, but Uncle Phillip's words of wisdom stayed with me. He taught me to always stay humble and to share the knowledge that I had so that it could benefit others.

This value of humility and knowledge-sharing was instilled in me from a young age, through my faith and the teachings of my parents. It was a core belief that guided me throughout my career, and it continues to shape my life and work today.

I remained in close contact with Uncle Phillip over the years, and I was devastated to learn that he had been diagnosed with a terminal illness - cancer. While cancer may seem like a commonplace disease in today's world, when it strikes someone you know and love, it can be a truly humbling and sobering experience.

For me, it was as though dark clouds had descended upon my world, and I found myself struggling to come to terms with the reality of the situation. As I grappled with my emotions and tried to process the news, I was struck by the fragility of life and how quickly everything can change.

The days that followed were filled with deep reflection, and I found myself pondering the mysteries of life and our ultimate destiny. It was a challenging time, but it also served as a reminder to cherish every moment we have on this earth and to live each day with purpose and intention.

Six months after Uncle Phillip's diagnosis, I found myself sitting alone on a gloomy afternoon, reminiscing about his beautiful soul over a cup of tea. Suddenly, my phone rang, and the news I had been dreading finally came - Uncle Phillip had passed away.

Although I knew his illness was terminal, the news was still difficult to swallow. It felt as though a piece of me had been lost forever. However, even in the midst of my grief, I found solace in the fact that Uncle Phillip's legacy would live on. His beautiful soul and all the good he had done in the world would always be remembered.

As I thought about his life and the impact he had on mine, I realized that the greatest gift Uncle Phillip gave me was his belief in my potential. He saw something in me that I didn't see in myself, and he encouraged and supported me every step of the way. It was this belief and support that helped me achieve success in my career and in life.

Even though Uncle Phillip is no longer with us, his memory and his teachings will continue to inspire me and guide me on my journey. I am forever grateful for the gift of his presence in my life and the legacy of love and wisdom he left behind.

About Kennedy Albar

A passionate educator with a love for English and a strong belief in lifelong learning.

Email: kennedyalbar@hotmail.com

13

Suria – Truly A Beautiful Soul

Hadi Al Maatiin

In my life, many people have come and gone, leaving behind their own unique imprint. Yet, there is one individual who has made an indescribable impact on my journey. Her name is Kak Suria, my mentor and guiding light. Through her wise counsel and unwavering support, I have undergone a transformation that has brought me to a place of greater love and understanding. Kak Suria has witnessed my growth and has been an instrumental part of my personal development journey. I feel so blessed to have met her and to continue to learn from her shining example of what it means to be a Beautiful Soul.

"You are a born leader, given how you fulfill your role as Program Director. You are destined to be a star and not to be working at the airport. I see you as a motivational speaker, a hero, and a leader who will guide and inspire others. I don't usually say this to everyone, but I feel that this message is meant for you and your clear vision. To make this happen, start receiving effortless success gracefully, okay? Anything that comes easily to you, accept it without pushing it away with guilt."

Years ago, these were the words of encouragement that she spoke to me when I set out on a new path of self-discovery and personal growth. At the time, I was going through a period of inner turmoil that had been building up for months. Despite being only thirty-five years old, I felt haggard and burned out. I was struggling to find my way, both physically and emotionally, and my self-worth had been shattered after a broken engagement. But I was determined to search for inner strength and regain my sense of dignity and purpose, so that I could rise again and move forward in my life.

I first met Kak Suria in person when I joined a network marketing program through an old friend. I was determined to turn my life around, to take control of my destiny. At first, I was hesitant to participate in any events or gatherings because of my shame and lack of self-confidence. I felt like a born loser, and I was afraid of being seen in public or group meetings. But with Kak Suria's guidance and support, I achieved one breakthrough after another over the past five years. She helped me regain my confidence and showed me that I could overcome any obstacle if I believed in myself.

Thanks to the Genius IQ program, I managed to transform from a "lion-dad" to a Positive Parent Advocate. The Money Detox program helped me rid myself of heavy debts-guilt and my problems with money and wealth. Through the Speed Slim program, I lost weight, learned about nutrition and natural healing. The Soul of Success program taught me about the Emotional Freedom Techniques, and I made peace with my inner self. Kak Suria's mindset training even helped me quit smoking for over a year. But that's not all. I also achieved other breakthroughs such as being selected to facilitate events. From my previous roles as audio and usher, I was chosen to be an emcee and speak publicly on stage.

At first, the thought of being an emcee was terrifying because it was my biggest fear. However, with Kak Suria's trust and belief in me, I applied the mindset skills she taught me. From that moment on, I discovered that I truly enjoyed being an emcee. One day, I was nominated to be the Assistant Program Director, working alongside my coach-turned-wife Teeya, who was the Program Director for that month. I continued to support other Program Directors in the following months, and soon Kak Suria entrusted me with the responsibility of being a Program Director for the first time at a Facebook Marketing event. Despite having no experience in running events, let alone big ones, it turned out to be the highlight of my journey. I nailed it, and those warm words from my mentor were a testament to my success.

Kak Suria taught me self-healing techniques that opened the door to a journey of self-discovery. Under her guidance, I learned the true meaning of forgiveness. I discovered the power of forgiving not just others, but also myself for the mistakes I had made. By practicing forgiveness, I was able to let go and allow God to perform miracles in my life. Forgiving others and myself lightened the burden I had been carrying for so long.

Kak Suria is a truly selfless leader who goes above and beyond the duties of a coach. She exemplifies this by helping me launch my online business through social media and coaching me throughout the entire presentation. Her unwavering support and willingness to share her thoughts and ideas have been invaluable to me. Her positive energy is contagious, and there have been occasions when I felt really down, but after meeting her, I always feel recharged and re-energized.

Kak Suria has been a constant source of encouragement in my dream of becoming an author. She motivates me to transform my thoughts into writing and inspired me to write every day. Thanks to her unwavering support, I have been able to write consistently and even post my writing on social media. What began as a passion has now become a habit, and this habit has ultimately transformed into a lifestyle.

I had always longed for a big sister, and I believe that God answered my prayers through Kak Suria. Her presence in my life has empowered me to become a better human being and has helped me mature in dealing with life's challenges and obstacles. I am grateful and blessed to have met her, and I thank God for bringing her into my life.

About Hadi Al Maatiin

Hadi aspires to be a published author. He has just embarked on a new journey as a Debt Restructuring Associate, helping people become debt-free through the government program DRS. For a complimentary consultation, please fill out the form: https://tinyurl.com/bedebt-freenow

Follow him on his Facebook page:

https://www.facebook.com/profile.php?id=100063958845804&mibextid=ZbWKwL

14

My Father, My Hero

Dr. Yolanda Hiew

Some of us may not realize that in a lifetime, we admire others who may be successful, rich, healthy, happy, and have lots of freedom to do whatever they want. People who are closest to us, such as our parents, can be easily ignored for their strengths, good deeds, and achievements. In my life, I get motivated by various individuals in my day-to-day existence. Despite being inspired by numerous things, I have someone who inspires me the most - my father.

The doctor gave my papa three months to live after his diagnosis of a tumour that grew on his kidney. Despite that, he refused surgery and outlived the disease for nine years! His mentality was still strong, although his condition worsened day by day two months before his passing at the age of 84.

Papa did not want the operation as suggested by the specialists, and he was 75. My brother and I took turns explaining the surgery to Papa, but he refused to be admitted. We sought second and third opinions from different specialists, and all came back with the same advice - the only way for Papa to survive was to have surgery to remove the lump. Papa said that in our lifetime, we cannot live with only one kidney, and there would be some form of imbalance in the human body function. Although he only studied up to primary education, he read the Chinese newspaper daily. His knowledge came from reading and personal experience, apart from his wisdom from his background in kung-fu.

As a young kid, I often spoke loudly in Papa's ear as he could not hear properly. His eardrum was damaged when he was in his mid-40s, and my older sister got him a hearing aid years later. However, he eventually stopped using it. He worked hard to support us, always with a smile on his face, and never scolded me or my siblings. I guess it might be because of his outstation job and being rarely at home, where I saw him every few months while growing up. There was a time when he brought home a puppy, and for the first time, I had a puppy to play with every day after school.

At some point, I observed Papa's daily routine. He used to sleep at 10 in the night and got up at 5 in the morning. Then, he would have a cold shower before going to the market, which was just a ten-minute walk, to buy groceries and cook lunch and dinner for us. He would enjoy his breakfast and read his newspapers in the morning. I always felt so secure whenever I was with Papa, be it at home or other places, as he had a strong energy. Even though he is no longer with us, I still feel like I'm my Papa's little girl.

The growth in Papa's kidney came as a shock to me and my family. Hence, we discussed his old age and existing hypertension to determine whether he should carry on with the surgery. Nevertheless, Papa let go of the idea of surgery and decided to leave it as it was. He did his own thing to change and maintain a healthy lifestyle, and self-remedy was often his trademark. Apart from our help in getting him the fruits and vegetables he needed, Papa would go for brisk walks every morning from home to the nearby park. Moreover, his Kung-Fu background and positive mindset could be the main reasons for his survival and the decision not to remove the growing tumour, which was the size of a golf ball in his initial diagnosis.

Papa was living his normal life, knowing that he had cancer, and tried to quit smoking several times. Once in a while, he enjoyed some liquor while watching his favorite sports on TV by himself. He was independent and looked after himself as well as us and my mum for years since his retirement at age 60. Papa loved cooking and making delicious traditional village cakes, and whenever we had a family gathering, he would cook his favorite soup while Mum cooked her chicken dish. He cooked authentic Chinese dishes for us and played with his grandchildren whenever they visited him. He was also an energetic and caring grandpa.

I remember whenever friends and relatives met Papa, they would ask how he was doing, and Papa would always give a thumbs up to indicate he was doing very well. Although members of my family did not reveal Papa's health condition to anyone, most of our relatives treated Papa as a normal and strong person. From the outside, his hearing impairment might not have appeared to affect his way of life. I believe that his livelihood would have been better and he could have been more successful if he could hear. I always knew that Papa would have been a great scholar if he continued his education because of his intelligence and positive mentality.

As a teenager, Papa had encouraged me to study hard and made sure I did my homework after school. During my first year of secondary school, I used to do my homework on the dining table, and some time later, Papa surprised me with a study desk as a gift. I felt the love; Papa didn't just say things to encourage me, but he took action to show me he really cared. As years went by, I left Malaysia for England to chase after my dreams. I made a promise to Papa and Mum that I would come back as a graduate. Ten years later, I returned after achieving a master's degree and with my bundle of joy, my baby girl.

After returning from England with my eight-month-old daughter, my Mum looked after her, and Papa would play with her every day. He bought many exercise books and taught my daughter to draw. I was busy at work and did not have much time except on weekends when I brought them for a day out at the beach and back home for dinner. As a single mother and young widow, Papa had been a father figure to my daughter.

While I was busy with my PhD at the local university, I literally forgot about the growth in Papa's kidney. It was because he did not seem like he had cancer, and he never returned to the hospital for follow-up tests. Papa was given 3-6 months to live. I knew I had to make him proud by finishing my PhD. Regrettably, he passed away just weeks before my convocation ceremony, for which I had booked two tickets for him and Mum to attend. However, I was lucky to insist on taking the graduation photo at the studio a few months before the convocation took place.

Although Papa had a hearing impairment, he was quite concerned about his health. Not only was he healthy and strong when he was young until his last breath, but he was also passionate about martial arts and had learned Traditional Chinese Medicine. As a teenage boy and one of the eldest boys in the family, Papa came to the city to work and survived on his own. I learned from Papa how to take care of my health too. I remember Papa telling me that we all need to keep moving our bodies, especially by walking. In his 80s, he could walk without any assistance, cook, read, and enjoy anyone's company.

In 2016, nine years after the first diagnosis, Papa fell ill due to breathlessness. My brother and I brought him back to the same private hospital to see the specialist. His health deteriorated over the span of three weeks, and he was admitted in and out of the hospital several times. By that time, Papa's tumor had grown to the size of a tennis ball. He experienced difficulty breathing due to liquid in his lungs, and the doctor informed us that the cancer had spread to his lungs as well. Finally, Papa was admitted to the hospital. The doctor was surprised to see Papa's medical record, as he had lived much longer than expected from his initial diagnosis, which was nothing short of a miracle.

Papa greatly impacted my life, and I was still learning from him in his final months before he passed away. Throughout my childhood, I always heard him say, 'your studies are more important than anything' and 'do not hold grudges towards others; always keep the peace.' I admire Papa for his bravery and positive mentality towards life and in handling crises. Although he may not have been a perfect father, to me, he was a kind, caring, patient, friendly, knowledgeable, and disciplined person who could take care of himself without his children and wife worrying about him.

Most of all, my beloved father was a great survivor and will always be my hero. With his wisdom, I will forever cherish and keep in mind what he said to me when I was about to complain about others. Papa said, 'Life will not be peaceful if we hold grudges against one another.'

Rest in peace, Papa. You will always be my hero.

About Dr Yolanda Hiew

Dr Yolanda Hiew is an author, educator, and health coach who is inspired by her father's legacy. She helps students excel in their studies through her book 'Be A Graduate', and transforms lives by promoting fitness and health.

https://www.facebook.com/Yolanda.Hiew

www.ingramcontent.com/pod-product-compliance
Lightning Source LLC
LaVergne TN
LVHW050326160826
845677LV00014B/3546

9789811871139